AF269728

★ ALL-TIME ★
BEST ATHLETES

PRO WRESTLING SUPERSTARS

PERCY LEED

LERNER PUBLICATIONS ◆ MINNEAPOLIS

Lerner Publications Company
An imprint of Lerner Publishing Group, Inc.
241 First Avenue North
Minneapolis, MN 55401 USA

For reading levels and more information, look up this title at www.lernerbooks.com.

Main body text set in Mikado.
Typeface provided by HVD Fonts.

Library of Congress Cataloging-in-Publication Data

Names: Leed, Percy, 1968– author.
Title: Pro wrestling superstars / Percy Leed.
Description: Minneapolis : Lerner Publications, [2024] | Series: Lerner sports rookie. All-time best athletes | Includes bibliographical references and index. | Audience: Ages 5–8 years | Audience: Grades K–1 | Summary: "Pro wrestling features some of the most recognizable names in sports history. But how many are legendary? Check out the top ten best wrestlers in pro wrestling history and how they earned their spots"– Provided by publisher.
Identifiers: LCCN 2023036866 (print) | LCCN 2023036867 (ebook) | ISBN 9798765625743 (lib. bdg.) | ISBN 9798765628201 (pbk.) | ISBN 9798765632444 (epub)
Subjects: LCSH: Wrestling—Juvenile literature. | Wrestlers—Rating of—Juvenile literature. | World Wrestling Entertainment, Inc.—Juvenile literature.
Classification: LCC GV1195.3 .L44 2024 (print) | LCC GV1195.3 (ebook) | DDC 796.812092/2 [B]—dc23/eng/20231018

LC record available at https://lccn.loc.gov/2023036866
LC ebook record available at https://lccn.loc.gov/2023036867

Manufactured in the United States of America
2-1012337-51908-3/10/2026

TABLE OF CONTENTS

Turn the pages to meet the best pro wrestlers. Count them down from **10** to **1**. Number 1 is the best pro wrestler ever!

10. TRISH STRATUS

Trish Stratus was famous for her Stratusfaction move. She used it to end many matches.

COUNT IT!

WWE Women's Championships: 7

Trish Stratus

9. BRUNO SAMMARTINO

Bruno Sammartino was a top wrestler.

His strength and size made him

tough to beat.

8. SHAWN MICHAELS

Shawn Michaels was a rough and strong fighter. He won the Royal Rumble in 1995 and 1996.

"Macho Man" Randy Savage

7. "MACHO MAN" RANDY SAVAGE

"Macho Man" Randy Savage pumped up crowds with his high energy. He knocked out wrestlers using his famous moves.

6. DWAYNE "THE ROCK" JOHNSON

Dwayne "the Rock" Johnson had two famous moves, the Rock Bottom and the People's Elbow.

COUNT IT!
WWE
Championships: 8

Dwayne "the Rock" Johnson

5. MANAMI TOYOTA

Manami Toyota had exciting matches. In one of them, the loser had to shave their head. Toyota won!

4. BRET "THE HIT MAN" HART

Bret "the Hit Man" Hart once beat Steve Austin when Austin was a heel. Austin became a babyface after the match. Hart became a heel.

Bret "the Hit Man" Hart
ROUGEAU

18

3. HULK HOGAN

Hulk Hogan was a superstar. He had his own TV shows. He wrestled stars such as Ric Flair, the Rock, and André the Giant.

2. "STONE COLD" STEVE AUSTIN

"Stone Cold" Steve Austin often scared other wrestlers. He once used a chair to fight against the Rock.

COUNT IT!

WWF Tag Team Championships: 4

1. RIC FLAIR

Ric Flair had strength and skill. His leglock is one of the best moves of all time.

COUNT IT!

NWA World Heavyweight Championships: 8

NOW IT'S YOUR TURN.

Who do you think are the best pro wrestlers of all time? Make your own list!

GLOSSARY

babyface: the good guy, or the wrestler people often root for in a match

heel: the bad guy, or the wrestler people often root against in a match

leglock: when a wrestler wraps their legs around another wrestler, locking them between their legs and body

LEARN MORE

Arnez, Lynda. *Be a Pro Wrestler*. Buffalo: Gareth Stevens, 2024.

Miller, Marie-Therese. *34 Amazing Facts about Pro Wrestling*. Minneapolis: Lerner Publications, 2024.

Rose, Rachel. *Dwayne Johnson: Actor and Pro Wrestler*. Minneapolis: Bearport, 2022.

INDEX